Crossing Over

A Poetry Collection

Heidi Ritzel

Dedication

For my parents, who bravely crossed an ocean in search of a better life. They are the true definition of the American Dream.

And for my husband Bill: my beloved, my soulmate, my best friend. I adore him now and for all eternity.

Acknowledgements

I would like to thank the writers who have inspired me: Elizabeth Gilbert, Cheryl Strayed, Billy Collins, Sylvia Plath, Mary Oliver, Jenny Lawson, and F. Scott Fitzgerald. They are all true masters of their craft.

I offer towering mountains of gratitude for those who have encouraged my writing: Patti Aha, Randy Peterson, Pete Diercksen, Pat Diercksen, Christine Wessels Smith, Sonja Reed, Michela Backman, and Debbie Rosmus. Two special teachers deserve mention here as well. My high school English teacher Miriam Jacobson, who planted the seed that I had some talent, and Dr. Richard Simpson, one of my professors at St. Bonaventure University, who watered that seed until it grew into a towering tree of belief in my writing ability. If there is anyone I have neglected to mention who has encouraged me along my creative journey, I offer heartfelt gratitude to you as well.

Huge hugs go out to my husband Bill, who thinks everything I write is wonderful and should be published. Thank you, my love.

And for my parents, who inspired the poems in this book. When I first dreamed of becoming a writer, I promised I would dedicate my first book to them. This book is for you, Mom and Dad. I hope my words have made you proud.

Preface

Poems are snapshots. Moments brought to life with description, imagery, and emotion. Poems provide a glance into a moment in time that may otherwise be forgotten. They have the extraordinary ability to move the reader into the writer's world.

My parents were German immigrants. They came to the United States on a ship in 1954 with nothing but their clothes, my mother's sewing machine, and the most precious thing they had: my brother. The poems contained in this book are poetic snapshots of my parents and their journey cobbled together from stories I heard throughout my life. It is also about the experience from my perspective as the daughter of immigrants and how it shaped my life.

I hope these poems provide a snapshot into both my life and that of my parents as they searched for and came to epitomize the American Dream.

Voyage

She kneels on the deck of the ship.
Tailored blouse, proper shoes, churning
stomach.
To her right is a baby boy
cooing to the rhythm of the waves
as she changes his diaper.
To her left is the bucket that holds
the remains of her breakfast.
She reaches down and picks up her boy,
holds him close.
She is shaking against the chill of the Atlantic
and the fear of all that will follow.
For nine days this routine has become
familiar in its horror.
Diaper, vomit, diaper, vomit.
She doesn't believe her stomach will ever
recover.

Her husband joins her.
He looks out at the water with nervous
anticipation of his new life
in the new world.
Her stomach tosses up the last of her toast.

She is terrified of change,
of the people who will speak to her
in a language she does not understand,
of the judgment she feels sure will follow.

Day ten arrives.
She empties her bucket,
changes another diaper.
In the distance she sees something.
Only a shadow at first
but it looms large before her.
Soon a statue is visible, a lady with a torch
welcoming them to their new homeland.
The man smiles.
The woman cries.

The American Dream awaits.

Beginnings

The chickens never stopped laying eggs.
My mother was tired, so tired,
from the baby boy who needed constant
attention to working nonstop
in the egg cellar of the chicken farm,
putting eggs into the correct slots,
throwing away the bad ones.
But both her baby's needs and those eggs
just never stopped.

My dad had it easier.
Out in the sun he plowed the fields, fed the
chickens, fixed tractors, mowed grass,
made minor repairs on the chicken farm's
buildings.
His job was busy but constantly changing
and he didn't have to worry about the baby.

He had something bigger to worry about:
money.
First there was the $1,250 that he owed my
mother's uncle for sponsoring them
to come to America.

He paid that off in one year.
Then it was on to buying a house,
a fixer upper before that was even a term.
With hard work and time,
that house became the most beautiful in our
small town,
my folks taking endless pride in their flower
and vegetable gardens,
turning a worn-down house into a home.

The Apprentice

My father had trained to be a farm manager
in Germany.
Before he was drafted into the war,
he worked on a large farm as an apprentice.
The farm grew mostly sugar beets
and my dad had twenty men to supervise.
As they labored in the fields,
he worked with them,
learning every aspect of farm management
along the way.
At noon, while the farmhands got their grub,
my father was required to go into the large
farmhouse,
change as if for a fancy meal,
eat a proper dinner,
change back into his work clothes,
and finish out the day's work.

The woman of the house sat at the head of
that table,
commanding and demanding respect
while gazing down her nose at the very
people who made her wealth possible.

She was difficult, demanding, and never
stopped reminding her workers
Wo ich sitze ist oben.
Where I sit is the top.
I am certain this is why my dad
was never impressed by money or status.

After the war, after meeting my mom,
after coming to America, after paying his
dues on the chicken farm,
my dad spent his life as a simple carpenter.
He was good at it and seemed content,
yet I have always wondered if he had dreams
of living in the American West
where he could have used his specialized
knowledge on a ranch
instead of being a carpenter in a small town
in New York state.

Did he dream of cows and horses
instead of hammers and saws?

Tailored

My mother had two jobs in Germany.
She worked as a secretary,
then apprenticed to become an expert tailor.
Her sewing was perfection.
No seam crooked, no button that missed its
companion hole, no uneven hems.
She made a few dollars a week by taking in,
letting out, and hemming clothing
for the women in our rural New York state
town.

When I was a teenager my parents bought me
a used sewing machine.
The idea of making my own clothes thrilled
the creative part of me.
We went to the fabric store and I selected a
pattern and some fabric.
My mom showed me how to use the machine,
and soon I was on my bedroom floor,
pinning the tissue-paper thin pattern
to my fabric.
I cut it out, pinned it, sewed it together.
I couldn't wait to show my mother.

But my seams were not perfect.
Rip them out and do it again, she demanded.
My hem was uneven.
Do it again.
The finished product looked nothing like the
picture.
You need to make it again.
Sewing, it seemed, was not something I was
tailored for.

Fifty years later I imagine how nice it would
be to make simple alterations to my clothes.
But no sewing machine will ever be in my
house because I know my mother's voice
would accompany it,
and my ever-wavering self-esteem
would sink lower than those patterns
on my teenage bedroom floor.

Hiding

Let's go, she said in an annoying stage whisper.
Without waiting for me to move,
she grabbed my arm
and ushered me across the living room
into the space between the drapes and the
couch where she made me
crouch down and hide.
Shhh! She demanded.
My mother stood behind the drapes,
nervous energy pouring down on me as we
waited.
The cause of this reaction was a car that had
parked in our driveway.
I raised my body just far enough so my eyes
were above the windowsill.
Two people got out of the car and were
heading toward our front door.
Shhh! She said again.
Then we waited.

Our unwelcome strangers walked past the
window in front of where we were hiding,

rounded the corner and approached
our front door.
From a small window next to the door,
we could see them as they climbed
the three steps to the door,
which meant that they could also see us.
My mother shifted the drapes to hide us
better.
They knocked, waited, knocked again.
We watched them retreat to their car,
then proceed down our driveway and onto
the road.
My mother was visibly terrified.
For several minutes we waited.
In case they come back, my mother said.
Finally, she let me go back
to my favorite chair
while she opened the front door.
Several pamphlets fell out when she did.
The unwelcome guests were Jehovah's
Witnesses,
harmless people sent out to spread God's
word.

I wonder who my mother imagined they
were.
Was there a PTSD element from the war at
play here?
Did she think the Gestapo was after her?
I'll never know,
but I carry this inherited fear with me,
unwilling to allow others in
while standing behind drapes of my own
creation.

Translation Required

I met my mother's parents three times
and my father's parents twice.
But I couldn't talk to them,
these Omas and Opas of mine.
Awkward conversations were conducted
with my parents as translators
and me nodding and smiling sweetly.
What were they saying?
These adults with whom I shared a bloodline
couldn't understand me any more than
I could understand them.

It's an odd thing to realize
that people from across an ocean
who speak a foreign language
and bring you little German dolls
could possibly be related to you.

I wish I could have had real conversations
with them.
To understand them would have been
to comprehend more
of where my parents came from

and where I came from as well.
Instead they chatted with my parents
as I sat on the sidelines
both bored and awed by their
incomprehensible conversations.

No Tears

The phone rang at five in the morning.
Even in my tiny upstairs bedroom
the shrill sound of the kitchen phone
pierced the morning air and annoyed my
tired brain.
Calls this early in the day were always from
Germany.
One set of grandparents or the other,
trying to catch my parents before they went
to work.
My Opa had fallen from a cherry tree several
days earlier,
and my dad was quite worried.
I thought this would be the call telling us he
was dead.
But the universe pulled the ultimate
bait and switch.
My dad hung up the phone and said,
My mother is dead. Heart attack.
Then he got dressed, ate his Rice Chex cereal,
and went to work.

That afternoon he came home early to take
me to the dentist
because my mother did not drive.
My mother looked at him and sneered,
What's wrong with your eyes?
I looked at my dad, always so strong and
brave,
and saw the ocean of tears he had been
holding back since five a.m.
Sawdust, he said. *There's sawdust in my eyes.*
Even at nine years old,
I knew this lie was meant to keep my
mother's disapproval of emotions at bay.
But looking deeply into my father's
sorrow-filled eyes
from the backseat of a Chevy
on a rainy day drive to the dentist's office
was the moment I discovered empathy.

Culinary Delights

My mother was an adequate cook.
Our meals were simple: boiled potatoes with
a bit of salt,
vegetables from our garden in the summer
and a can in the winter,
and meat, almost always chicken or pork.
Aside from the salt in the potato water,
she never used spices
and no one seemed to mind
because we didn't know any better.
My dad's only desire was that meat and
potatoes were on the table
every night when he got home from work at
five o'clock.
He was hungry and ate greedily,
his small sandwich long gone from his
stomach.

My food choices were limited and never
varied.
I never tasted peanut butter until I was in
college.

Mayo never crossed my lips either.
Or shrimp or sweet potatoes.
There was no ice in our house,
much to the amazement of visitors
who preferred their beverages cold
instead of room temperature.
My mom's idea of spaghetti
was elbow macaroni topped
with a jar of Ragu.
She cooked farina and we ate it as a dessert,
cold and topped with raspberry jam.

But baking is where her talent shined.
She was always scouring women's magazines
for recipes,
trying them out on us first, baking them
again when company came.
She always thought what she made was
horrible and a mistake,
but I never tasted anything she baked that
wasn't amazing.

Her mother also liked to bake,
and this love was passed along to me.
Now whenever I mix batter for muffins

or dive my hands into a mound
of scone dough,
I know a rich heritage of bakers is gazing over
my shoulder,
smiling with approval at every item that
emerges from my oven.

Accented

I lived with my parents for the first 18 years
of my life and heard them speak every day.
People would comment that they had accents.
Ignorant classmates would say they talked
funny.
But I never heard my parents' accents until
the first time
I called them from college.

When they dropped me off at my
small Franciscan university
five hours away from home,
they told me to call collect
every other Sunday night.
Long distance phone calls were expensive
back then,
and my parents had no money for idle
conversation.
Two weeks later I sat in the little seat in the
telephone booth
in the common section of my dorm.
I figured out how to call collect
and a man answered.

A man with an accent.
Then he handed the phone to a woman
who also had an accent.
Were the people on the other end of the
phone really my parents?
I don't know how to explain this
phenomenon other than to believe that
because I heard their voices every day
their accents were just a part
of who they were.
Familiar.
But I came away from that first phone call a
changed person.
The proud immigrants who raised me
really did speak English with the strong
accent of a faraway country.
Of that I would always be proud.

Drowning

I am drowning
slipping deeper
flailing my arms
needing you to pull me up.
You held me inside before I was born,
knew me before I had a name
and let go as soon as I began life.
You love from a distance now,
cradle me through a telephone line,
never say the words.
I am a child with you
still wanting to be held.
I am an adult without you
unable to feel the love you never gave.
I need to please everyone
just to please you.
Why do you leave me sinking
without ever teaching me to swim?

Wanderlust

My mother had a serious case of stifled
wanderlust.
My father, ever the pragmatist concerned
about money,
didn't believe travel was worth the cost.
But in her comfortable chair in the living
room next to my dad,
she could watch travel shows,
read magazine articles,
dream of all the places she wanted to see.

Their 50th wedding anniversary
was coming up.
Would they like a party or a trip?
My brother and I would pay for whatever
they wanted.
No party, but they would love a trip.
I was certain they would want to travel
back to Germany one more time,
but my mother had other plans.
She wanted to see the Canadian Rockies.
My husband and I decided it would be easier
and safer for them if we went along.

But this was only months after the horror of
9/11 and no one wanted to get on a plane.
We'll drive! My husband offered.
And we did.
West through four Canadian provinces,
awed by the beauty of the Rockies,
then back east through nine U.S. states.
Three weeks total.

My mother was not easy to travel with.
She refused to say that she needed a
bathroom break.
She would not verbalize wanting food or
water.
And yet the photo album she created of that
trip illustrated her delight
at having witnessed such beauty firsthand.
For years, she talked about the mountains,
the things we did, the people we met.
The driving we did.
The joy she felt.

I finally understood that for my mom,
traveling itself was only a third of her joy.

The other two thirds were the anticipation of
the trip and the fond reminiscing
of seeing something she had only dreamed of.

Crossing Over

Did you think it would change
when you crossed the waters?
You held your baby boy close
as sea mist carried away memories
you claimed didn't exist.
Seventy years later they
are locked within you still
like a precious heirloom,
ghosts of a faraway country
whose language sounds foreign to you now.
If you could have fast-forwarded your life,
would you have done more to
escape the demons
that rage in your mind?
There are days when sunlight
fires your nerve endings
and you scurry about
as if fed intravenously with caffeine.
But the sun doesn't always rise
and sometimes each breath you exhale
expels a small corner of your soul
in tiny droplets of water
carried off by the breeze.

The baby you held so tightly
holds court in your life.
The one who came later
was purged from your body
to cast an unwelcome shadow
in your search for the light.
She has remained in darkness,
eating so the pounds will hide her,
withholding her voice
so the silence can blanket her,
disappearing further
into nothingness
as you did,
looking for an ocean to cross.

Life on Hold

I was a diner waitress for six years
after receiving my English degree.
To my parents' credit,
they never told me I was wasting my life
or needed to find a real job.
They knew this *was* a real job.
It was a hard job, the only waitress on the
three to eleven shift,
serving seven tables and a counter.
They knew I was in a holding pattern and
that being a waitress was not going to be my
life's work.
But did they wonder why only one of their
children had a decent job?

I felt an internal pressure to get a job
for which they would be proud,
but they never said a negative word about it.
I believe they knew that finding my true
calling was my own ocean to cross,
and that one day I would reach the shoreline
of a more stable life.

No Room of My Own

Between my sophomore and junior years in
college,
my parents built a house
with a small influx of cash
from my mother's parents' will.
They purchased six acres of land a mile
outside of our small town.
The plan was to build a house in the middle,
so no neighbor would ever be too close.
My dad and his carpentry partner would
build the house
with a little help from my brother and me.
I helped mix the cement for the foundation.
My brother had worked with our dad for
several summers,
so he provided help with an abundance of
tasks.
We all worked hard on that house
knowing it was the dream home our parents
always wanted.

But the home was built with the same layout
one would have in Germany.

The front door opened to a long hallway
and the rooms jutted off from there.
Sewing room, kitchen, dining room
to the left,
bedroom and bathroom to the right,
living room straight ahead.
It was an odd layout for an American home
but it was the interior they found most
comfortable.

I don't remember how I found out.
My college friend has a clear recollection
of my reaction and tears,
but I don't remember the actual finding out.
It was just something I feel like I always knew.
My parents built a house
with no room for me.
No guest room, no closet, no room for a
dresser or a daughter.
I would spend my time home from college
on an old twin-size bed in my father's gun
room.
Every morning I woke up
as deer heads looked down on me
with empathetic eyes.

At least they had a room of their own.

No Memories

I open the photo album slowly.
The pages crunch beneath my fingertips
as I turn page after page,
one aging photo after another,
faded black and white memories
perfectly stopping moments in time,
the blissful childhood
of an immigrant's son.

There he is in a crib.
Now he's growing up on the chicken farm,
riding shotgun on a tractor next to his father
surrounded by a litter of kittens,
holding a rake that's taller than he is
while hanging onto his mother's dress.
In each photo he is smiling with delight,
images of a blond boy taken by parents
who want to freeze these moments in time.

Fifty years later I scan these photos into my
computer.
This boy is my brother, and I smile at what a
lucky child he was.

Days come and go as I scan and scan,
an endless stream of happy smiles
in shades of gray.
Then I am done.

The next time I see my parents I ask my
mother where I am.
Where are the grainy pictures of my
childhood?
I burned them, she says without even a hint of
shame.
They were slides but I knew you wouldn't want
them anyway.
I cannot make myself speak.
I cannot make myself explain how slides can
be made into photos.
I cannot let myself cry in her presence.
I simply wait until she is out of sight,
then sob uncontrollably.

I imagine her at the oil drum she used to burn
our garbage
using the end of a broom handle to stir it,
the slides of me next to
junk mail, week-old newspapers,

and potato peels.
I spot a tiny corner of a slide
in which my six-year-old self is smiling.
I look happy.
I smile at the image before I cry
because I have never seen that look on my
face.
It was burned in an oil drum fifty years ago.

The Recording

I had wanted to record my father for years
and when I finally did,
he was open to answering all of my
well thought-out questions.
I walk him through what it was like in
Germany during the 20s and 30s
when he was growing up.
I ask about the war and he answers
matter-of-factly, honestly.
I quiz him about being in the war,
what it was like in a prisoner-of-war camp,
and coming back to his home.

My mom is ablaze with anger over what she
considers a stupid, useless exercise.
Why do you want to know all that? she hisses.
*It all happened so long ago it's not even true
anymore.*
But my mom always said this,
as though there is a statute of limitations on
the truth.
And for her, there always was.
Beyond her self-imposed time frame

of the past,
things simply had not happened.

But this recording, this history of my dad's
life, means more to me.
More to me than my mother's wrath.
More than her disapproval.
More than the attitude I will get for the next
three weeks when I call her.
I continue to ask the questions.
Each time she comes into the living room and
realizes my dad is speaking into the little
cassette recorder
that can hear her as well,
she says *I better shut up* and leaves the room.
Yet I keep asking questions.
My husband pipes in occasionally,
reinforcing what my dad has said.
Together they are two men exploring a past
that is part of me,
part of who I am but never quite understood.

In the recording his voice sounds the way
I will always remember it: strong and calm.
He recounts the story of his mother and aunt

taking his uncle to court over the sale of his
grandparents' house.
He describes his dad as being extremely
quiet.
He never said much, my dad recalls.
His mom, however, terribly upset that she
and her sister
got less than they were legally bound to get as
part of their parents' will
because numbers had been crossed out and
others handwritten in,
spoke up and hired a lawyer.
Then, this lawyer waited to settle the will
until after all the money in Germany, the
Reichsmark,
became useless overnight.
Because of this forward-thinking lawyer,
some money for my grandparents was
salvaged.

I listen more closely,
press the phone even more tightly to my ear.
It takes only these few minutes of tape
for me to understand the two sides of my
dad.

From his dad, quiet, steady.
From his mom, strong and loyal to her
family.
This was my dad.
Quiet, steady, strong, loyal.

My ear hurts now so I take the phone away
and press the pause button.
I am still here.
My dad is still gone.
His voice lingers in the air,
in the short distance between
the phone and my ear
in the space between this world and the next.

The Builder

I was the one with pen in hand
building imaginary worlds with words.
But my dad held the tools that built my life.
He formed the foundation for his young
immigrant family,
placing cinder block upon cinder block
cemented by love,
framing a house with two-by-four pieces of
integrity,
putting a roof over our heads
to shield us from the storms of life.

He hammered respect into me,
bolted a work ethic to my side,
drilled loyalty into me while ratcheting up my
honesty,
sawed off the pieces that hurt,
and sprinkled my life with kindness that fell
like sawdust.
Then he went into the world and built houses
and cabinets
and fixed anything that needed fixing,
building loyalty and trust in his community.

He kept building until the numbers on his
ruler morphed into rabbits
and the nails in his hand
became shiny bits of glitter,
his imagination growing bigger
as memories became smaller and more
distant.

Yet when the Lewy Bodies took over his
brain,
he continued to be the builder
reaching for hammers and screwdrivers and
nails that were now only in his mind.

I watch him alone in his room
pounding nails into the walls of his
imagination.
He reaches for tools he cannot find
so I pluck them out of the air
because I know right where they are.

As my foundation cracks under
the weight of my sorrow
he is still building.

I walk into the room,
pick up the sawdust of his mind
and sprinkle it over him,
a gentle shower of love
only the two of us can see.

Lunch With His Father

The lunch tray was perched on the table
before him.
My dad had developed a swallowing problem,
so the food on his plate was meat mush,
veggie mush, and potato mush.
There was also extra thick pudding
along with coffee and cranberry juice the
consistency of honey.
My husband and I sat with him,
our idle conversation paused so he could eat.

My dad reached out to the left of his tray,
grabbed something from the air, put it in his
mouth, and began chewing.
Then he reached for his imaginary juice and
began to talk,
so low that I could barely hear him,
but I know that he was speaking in German.
He was looking across the table
at an empty chair.
Who are you talking to? I asked.
My dad, he said, then smiled broadly and
continued talking.

We watched silently as my dad
ate an entire meal
visible only to him and the father he left
on the shore of Bremerhaven
more than 60 years earlier,
blissfully content that they could once again
share a meal.

The Lunchbox

In a forgotten corner of my parents' closet
I see a dark gray object that is so achingly
familiar
I don't even have to take it out to know what
it is.
It's my dad's lunchbox, the one he carried to
work every day.
I take it out of its hiding place, brush off the
dust, open it.
Suddenly I am thrown back to my childhood,
watching him leave the house every day with
that same lunchbox.
He had many over the years.
When one wore out he would buy an exact
replica.
His lunch was always the same:
A sandwich made with grainy bread
and some sort of cold meat, usually ham.
And coffee. Always coffee,
half for the morning coffee break and half to
drink with lunch.
I unscrew the Thermos and inhale

the aroma of coffee
forever embedded in the stainless steel.

I look at this box, untouched for so long,
and think of the man who carried it every
day.
From small jobs fixing a broken lock
or a hole in a wall
to building an entire house from the
foundation up,
wherever that lunchbox was, my dad was
nearby.
Someone who could always be relied on to do
carpentry work
with an eye toward perfection in every way.
His work ethic came along with that
lunchbox,
and opening it released a lifetime
of integrity, hard work, and pride.

Time and Time Again

What time is it? My mother asked,
over and over,
as I sat with her in the assisted living facility.
Two o'clock, I answered.
What time is dinner? Again, over and over.
Five o'clock, I answered with growing
impatience.
So what do I have to do now?
It was all I could do not to yell,
You're 90 years old! There is nothing you have to
do!
But I didn't. I couldn't.
Time had always been in charge,
stamping each phase of her life with numbers
to match the clock.
Time passed merrily as she walked home from
school with her friends in Germany,
laughing and stopping to tell stories,
the kind only young girls can giggle about.
Time stopped in its tracks as she and her
family hid in a bomb shelter
night after night during World War II,
wondering if they would survive.

Time ebbed and flowed with the ocean tide
as she, my dad, and my brother sailed to
America.
Time passed quickly as her son grew
and a daughter was added to the family.

I have been chased by time's inevitable march
as I rushed through a childhood
that should have been carefree.
Mine was ensnared in time.
Time was all around me.
Everywhere I gazed around my parents' living
room growing up,
there was a clock casting its judgmental eyes
upon me,
reminding me that there was always
something to do
somewhere to be
some task to be accomplished by a particular
time.
My entire life was one cosmic race against the
clock.
I became an extremely anxious adult,
spending four decades trying every
anti-anxiety medication in existence,

spilling my life story to therapists,
and spending an exorbitant amount of
money on meditation apps,
workshops, and books.
These attempts at saving myself from my own
mind were complete failures.

Yet that afternoon,
as my mother and I sat listening
to the relentless ticking of the clock in her
room,
I knew that she thought only of her next
deadline,
where she had to be, the next task to be done.
I was thinking of time as it moved my mom
along in her life.
She gazed at the clock counting the moments
to dinner.
I looked at this same clock and pondered
time as it counted down
the moments of her life.
Time had stopped for my dad a mere seven
months earlier.
My mom would die within a year of that day.
But that afternoon I was blissfully ignorant

of how little time I had left with her.
We watched time pass and as I saw this strong
woman overtaken by her obsession with time
even when there was nothing left to do,
I suddenly realized how much time she had
spent waiting for things that never happened.
Had I not been doing the same thing?
I had studied meditation, yearning to live in
the moment,
whispering the mantras,
counting my breaths,
trying to still my anxious mind,
but nothing had brought me to this point.
Watching someone I love allow her life to
pass with nothing
but angst over what was yet to come did it.
Suddenly the words of the meditation gurus
became as clear as the ticking of the clock.
We have only this moment. That's it.
I watched in awe as the to-do list in my mind
grew smaller and smaller
until it was one with the air around me
then it was gone.

As I grasped this sudden calmness over life's
larger questions,
my mother was content to stare at the clock
as it counted down to dinner.
I turned and we watched the clock together,
each lost in our own thoughts,
time whooshing by like an invisible tidal wave
carrying both our lives and our thoughts
out to an open, endless sea.

My Mother's Eyes

The blue of her eyes is all I notice.
Against the stark contrast of the
white hair, white pillowcase, white room,
her eyes are two clear glacial lakes
formed from mountains with snowy white
caps that melted, carrying with them a
lifetime of earthly particles borne of
angst and sorrow.

I gaze into these eyes,
envision her carrying me for nine months
before presenting me with a lifetime of
heartache.
She taught me not to cry
and I withheld tears
until my insides were a sea of sadness
and I could not swim to shore.
The things she did that hurt me, defined me,
challenged my sense of self,
made me feel like I was forever in her way
continue to hurt and I feel the sorrow,
yet I do not cry.

Through those eyes I see her soul,
the depths of love she could not give,
the strength of her will
to hold those feelings back.
I feel the pain in her clenched jaw,
a dam against emotions she would not feel.
I see it all now
clearly and deeply in those eyes.
But the hurt, the anger,
the grudge holding, the blame,
are all gone now,
whipped into a vortex of pure love.

The lakes of her eyes are receding
to a place I will no longer be able
to see them or feel their piercing pull.
I say goodbye, kiss her on the forehead.
She gazes at me with confusion
as one foot is already in the next world.

The next time I kiss her
she is cold and still
and I bleed tears like blood.

Embattled Blooms in a Plastic Bag

Next to the chair my mother would never sit
in again,
I found a bag of crocheted flowers
waiting to merge into an afghan.
Intricate petals with carefully selected colors
created night after lonely night
allowing a momentary quieting
of her anxious mind
that usually only the blare of the television
provided.
I imagine what they went through
on their way to being so lovely,
the battle each one faced while coming into
being.

I can see her, finishing a square,
holding it up to analyze its flaws
never stepping back to see
what beauty she had created.
A tiny crocheted flower and a daughter,
both held to the same scrutiny.

She looked at her work
as containing mistakes
and imperfections.
She saw only the flaws—a loose stitch, a few
extra pounds,
a person just making her way in the world as
herself,
a collection of blooms left to merge into a
comfortable blanket
but one that would never coalesce because she
left them.
The blooms, the daughter, all left behind to
wonder how they would ever become whole.

These would be the last to bloom, it turns out.
The last of many gardens
still waiting to come alive
in the spring of her death.

The Fabric of Life

Clothing tumbles through my fingers,
a tremendous dryer set on slow motion.
Work-worn flannel, silky polyester, rough
canvas.
I touch each one gently
press the fabric between my fingers
hold tight to the living and the dead.
In each thread a memory is embedded,
tiny moments I attempt to relive.

In the buttons of a plaid flannel shirt
I see my dad in his garden
tending the rows upon rows of potatoes
my mom will cook for dinner every night.
His denim overalls are stained with sweat,
still covered in sawdust from the last time he
wore them.
I find the knitted burgundy hat
he wore while plowing snow.
I hold it to my face and breathe in the pain of
his loss.

I feel my mother's anxiety as I touch

the neckline of the fuchsia dress
she wore to my wedding,
her anxiety palpable as she entered a world
where people belonged to country clubs
and owned two homes.
There is a neat row of mostly blue blouses,
polyester and wrinkle-free as they always
were because she hated to iron
but loathed wrinkles even more.

My dad's closet was that of a carpenter:
Work clothes, a few dress shirts for the
occasional dinner out,
one barely worn suit.
My mother had so many clothes,
and giving any of them away seems wrong.
I do it anyway.
These are only clothes, after all,
worn by the hard-working immigrants who
raised me,
now ready to be donated.

These are the clothes of two lives.
My parents' lives.
Only memories remain now.

But between each tiny thread,
no matter how ripped or well preserved,
there remains a part of their story.
I sort through those memories
as the clothes continue their sad tumble.
The clothes will soon be gone
but my memories are packed away in the
closet of my mind,
neat piles of my past woven together
like threads
entangling me with the sadness
of lives become dust.

The Visit

I stride toward the stone with purpose.
I have not been here in 15 months,
but now I'm on a mission.
My husband and I admire the stone,
a simple monument that would have met
with the approval
of both parties.
We wipe away some lawn clippings,
then he leaves me and I am alone with my
parents.

Hi. How are you doing?
I'm standing at the grave of my parents
talking to them the way I used to
when I called collect from college.
I have to hold myself back from asking
How's the weather there?
Instead I say that I miss them,
that I still cannot believe they are gone.
I feel my eyes begin to water
and I grab a tissue from my pocket,
press it against my eyes in an effort
to stuff the tears back in.

I tell my mom that I now understand
that she did what she knew how to do
that she was a product of her own upbringing
and did the best she could.
I tell her I love her and will forever
and that I forgive her for what she did
and for what she could not give me.
I'm sobbing now and the tissue is beginning
to shred.

Then I talk to my dad.
I tell him how I cherish
the time we spent together
when he taught me how to shoot a gun,
how to use a level,
how to measure twice and cut once,
how to mix the perfect vat of cement.
I tell him that the values he taught me by
example are how I try to live my life:
with integrity and trust, being true to my
word, being humble,
and above all else, being kind.

My tissue has now completely disintegrated.

I kiss my fingertips lightly,
then tap my hand gently on each of their
names.
I turn and walk toward my husband,
toward the rest of our day
toward the rest of a life
in which I will never again see my parents
but will always have them close to me
as I continue to feel their strong presence.
Their immigrant dream
and my current reality
now one.

Full Circle

August 2019.
I am in Bremerhaven, Germany,
standing on the rocky shoreline
in the exact spot
from which my parents' ship departed in 1954.
The fog forms drapes of gray.
I can hardly see the water
they would stare into for ten days,
yet from this spot I can feel my mother's fear
as she stepped onto the ship,
and my father's nervous anticipation
as he walked from the old world to a new one.

This was the beginning of their immigrant
journey,
the spot where before turned into after.
I tour the immigration museum in awed
silence,
marvel at the tiny cabins such tall people had
to endure,
view the exhibits that show where
the thousands of immigrants who sailed from
this port originated from

and where their journeys took them.

As I turn back to the car
the fog is slowly beginning to lift, and
a horizon of endless water comes into focus.
Millions of American Dreams began
in this spot.
My life is the result of one of those dreams,
the dreams of a terrified tailor
and a hopeful farmer,
sailing toward a better life.
I live within the richly woven fabric
of my heritage
in vivid shades of land and sky,
present with both past and future,
surrounded by endless oceans of gratitude.

www.ingramcontent.com/pod-product-compliance
Lightning Source LLC
LaVergne TN
LVHW021213200726
843509LV00012B/1434